„BÜCHER SIND WIE FALLSCHIRME.
SIE NÜTZEN UNS NICHTS, WENN
WIR SIE NICHT ÖFFNEN."

Gröls Verlag

Redaktionelle Hinweise und Impressum

Das vorliegende Werk wurde zugunsten der Authentizität sehr zurückhaltend bearbeitet. So wurden etwa ursprüngliche Rechtschreibfehler *nicht* systematisch behoben, denn kleine Unvollkommenheiten machen das Buch – wie im Übrigen den Menschen – erst authentisch. Mitunter wurden jedoch zum Beispiel Absätze behutsam neu getrennt, um den Lesefluss zu erleichtern.

Um die Texte zu rekonstruieren, werden antiquarische Bücher von Lesegeräten gescannt und dann durch eine Software lesbar gemacht. Der so entstandene Text wird von Menschen gegengelesen und korrigiert – hierbei treten auch Fehler auf. Wenn Sie ebenfalls antiquarische Texte einreichen möchten, finden Sie weitere Informationen auf www.groels.de

Viel Freude bei der Lektüre wünscht Ihnen das Team des Gröls-Verlags.

Adressen

Verleger: Sophia Gröls, Im Borngrund 26, 61440 Oberursel

Externer Dienstleister für Distribution & Herstellung: BoD, In de Tarpen 42, 22848 Norderstedt

Unsere „Edition | Werke der Weltliteratur" hat den Anspruch, eine der größten und vollständigsten Sammlungen klassischer Literatur in deutscher Sprache zu sein. Nach und nach versammeln wir hier nicht nur die „üblichen Verdächtigen" von Goethe bis Schiller, sondern auch Kleinode der vergangenen Jahrhunderte, die – zu Unrecht – drohen, in Vergessenheit zu geraten. Wir kultivieren und kuratieren damit einen der wertvollsten Bereiche der abendländischen Kultur. Kleine Auswahl:

Francis Bacon • Neues Organon • **Balzac** • Glanz und Elend der Kurtisanen • **Joachim H. Campe** • Robinson der Jüngere • **Dante Alighieri** • Die Göttliche Komödie • **Daniel Defoe** • Robinson Crusoe • **Charles Dickens** • Oliver Twist • **Denis Diderot** • Jacques der Fatalist • **Fjodor Dostojewski** • Schuld und Sühne • **Arthur Conan Doyle** • Der Hund von Baskerville • **Marie von Ebner-Eschenbach** • Das Gemeindekind • **Elisabeth von Österreich** • Das Poetische Tagebuch • **Friedrich Engels** • Die Lage der arbeitenden Klasse • **Ludwig Feuerbach** • Das Wesen des Christentums • **Johann G. Fichte** • Reden an die deutsche Nation • **Fitzgerald** • Zärtlich ist die Nacht • **Flaubert** • Madame Bovary • **Gorch Fock** • Seefahrt ist not! • **Theodor Fontane** • Effi Briest • **Robert Musil** • Über die Dummheit • **Edgar Wallace** • Der Frosch mit der Maske • **Jakob Wassermann** • Der Fall Maurizius • **Oscar Wilde** • Das Bildnis des Dorian Grey • **Émile Zola** • Germinal • **Stefan Zweig** • Schachnovelle • **Hugo von Hofmannsthal** • Der Tor und der Tod • **Anton Tschechow** • Ein Heiratsantrag • **Arthur Schnitzler** • Reigen • **Friedrich Schiller** • Kabale und Liebe • **Nicolo Machiavelli** • Der Fürst • **Gotthold E. Lessing** • Nathan der Weise • **Augustinus** • Die Bekenntnisse des heiligen Augustinus • **Marcus Aurelius** • Selbstbetrachtungen • **Charles Baudelaire** • Die Blumen des Bösen • **Harriett Stowe** • Onkel Toms Hütte • **Walter Benjamin** • Deutsche Menschen • **Hugo Bettauer** • Die Stadt ohne Juden • **Lewis Caroll** • *und viele mehr….*

Francis S. Betten

The Roman Index of Forbidden Books

Inhalt

SECTION I
COMMENTARY

1. The Index

In 1901, a reviewer of the Roman Index of Forbidden Books opened his criticism by congratulating himself upon having before him a genuine copy of that book, of which, he says, only a very limited number were printed for the exclusive use of "the leaders of the Church." Owing to its scarcity, he thinks, the owner of the volume, which he had borrowed, must have paid at least two hundred dollars for it. He could have bought a brand new copy for $2.25. The Index of which he speaks, issued by order of Leo XIII, in 1900, is for sale in this country by B. Herder, St. Louis, Mo. So are the three later editions (1901, 1904, 1907), the last two issued under, and by order of, our gloriously reigning Pontiff, Pius X. When the critic felt his heart beat with joy upon being allowed to view with his own blessed eyes a book so rare, so expensive, and so jealously guarded by "the leaders of the Church," a whole edition of that same book had already been sold, and a second was about to be put on the market. Its title is now:

Index librorum prohibitorum, Leonis XIII Sum. Pont. auctoritate recognitus SS. D. N. Pii P. X iussu editus. Præmittuntur Constitutiones Apostolicæ de examine et prohibitione librorum. (Index of forbidden books, revised by the authority of Pope Leo XIII, and issued by order of His Holiness Pope Pius X. Preceded by the Apostolic Constitutions on the examination and prohibition of books.)

A glance at the neatly printed volume will disclose the reason why it is called "Index";—almost nine-tenths of it consists of a catalogue of books condemned by the Roman authorities. Of still greater importance than this catalogue are the first thirty-four pages, which give, in the "Apostolic Constitutions," the general laws of the Church regarding books.

There are only two "Constitutions." But the whole work is introduced by a brief of Leo XIII, in which the Pontiff declares that this edition is to be the authentic one for the whole Church. *It is to be binding on all the faithful of the universe, regardless of race or language, nationality or country, education, learning or station in life.* In a preface headed "Lectori S.," the Secretary of the Roman "Congregatio Indicis" compares this edition of the "Index" with the former ones, points out the changes that were made, and explains the technical arrangement of the book.

After these preliminaries follow the "Constitutions." The first is the "Officiorum ac munerum" of Leo XIII, dated Jan. 25, 1896. This document recasts the whole legislation of the Church regarding the production, dissemination, reprinting and prohibition of such books as the Church may and must concern herself with. It abrogates all former laws and regulations of General Councils as well as of Sovereign Pontiffs, with one exception: the Constitution Sollicita ac provida of Benedict XIV, also reprinted here, by which this great pope established or rather sanctioned a method—the one still in use—of examining and passing sentence on the books submitted to the Roman authorities.

These two Constitutions contain the entire general legislation of the Church on the head of books.

There is no "Index expurgatorius." If there were, it would consist of books condemned conditionally, *donec corrigatur*, "until amended." But such books are all entered in the ordinary Index, with those two Latin words added. In Pope Leo's edition they are, besides, marked with an asterisk.

2. The Power of the Church

That the Church has the right to legislate on the publication and use of all books that touch on questions of faith and morals, must be evident to every Catholic. It is a truth clearly contained in the words of Christ to St. Peter: "Feed my lambs, feed my sheep," and in the duty imposed on the Apostles of "teaching the faithful to observe all, whatsoever I have commanded you."

The fact that general councils as well as many popes have issued laws and decrees regarding books, is sufficient evidence of their power and of their commission to do this. This very fact must also convince us that the observation of these laws must be salutary and conducive to the welfare of the Church at large and of the individual Christian.

The inventions, discoveries and progress of our times can introduce no change in this respect. The human mind is still as prone to err and as much subject to the persuasive influence of books as it ever was. Good books are as useful to-day as they were in olden times, and objectionable writings have the same deplorable effects they had a thousand years ago.

Nor can the Church, possessing the power to watch over our reading, neglect to make use of this power when the salvation of souls calls for its exercise. Bad literature is one of the worst enemies of mankind. The Church can never allow it to corrupt the hearts of her children or to undermine the foundation of their faith, without at least raising a warning voice.

How great are the precautions the civil authorities take in case of an epidemic; yet, no matter how seriously the precautions hamper traffic and trade, we find them reasonable. We should even censure our executive and legislative officers if they omitted to take proper precautions. But, says Pope Leo, in the Constitution Officiorum ac munerum, nothing can be conceived more pernicious, more apt to defile souls than uncurbed license in the writing and disseminating of bad books. "Therefore," he continues, "the Church, whose office it is to watch over the integrity of faith and morals, has ever striven, as far as in her power lay, to restrain the faithful from the reading of bad books as from a deadly poison."

3. Book Prohibitions Antedating the Roman Index

"The early days of the Church witnessed the earnest zeal of St. Paul," when the Christians at Ephesus brought together all the superstitious books they had in their possession and burned them publicly. This example of loyalty to the Church cost them, as Holy Scripture says, between eight and nine thousand dollars. Such was the policy in regard to bad books at Ephesus at a time when the Apostle whom many love to call the most liberal and broadminded, ruled that part of the Church.

Every subsequent age records similar measures of vigilance. The first General Council of Nicæa, in 325, besides proscribing the heresy of Arius, also issued a decree prohibiting the use of Arius' book Thalia, which contained his heresy; indeed, at all times the condemnation of a heresy by the Church entailed the prohibition of the works propagating it. Pope St. Leo the Great, 440–461, does not hesitate to declare that one who reads forbidden books cannot be considered a Catholic.

In the early days the Church had to direct her attention largely to the many so-called apocryphal books, falsely claimed to have been inspired by God and to form part of Holy Scripture. In 496, Pope Gelasius issued his famous decree, in which he enumerates the true books of the Bible, a number of the writings of the Fathers, (which he recommends,) together with a short list of apocryphal and heretical books, the reading of which he forbids.

In 745, by order of the Pope, a Roman synod examined and forbade a number of superstitious books sent by St. Boniface, who had found them among the Germans.

In fact, already in those days the entire present-day book legislation of the Church existed in all its essential features, though there were few written decrees. It seems the loyal Christian's duty of avoiding bad books, and the power of the Church to prohibit them, were held to be so self-evident that the need of written laws was not felt.

The necessity of watching over the mental food of the faithful became more urgent when, in the fifteenth century, was invented *printing*, which popes and bishops hailed as a "divine art" and eulogised as the greatest blessing of God's providence in the natural order. It spread rapidly. Before the year 1500, the city of Rome alone had one hundred and ninety printing establishments. The oldest of them, in the first seven years of its existence, produced not less than twenty-eight works in forty-seven editions, the total number of pages being one hundred and twenty-four millions.

As to the moral quality of the books printed at that period, a German, Wimpheling, writes with pardonable pride in 1507: "We Germans practically control the whole intellectual market of civilized Europe; *the books, however, which we bring to this market are for the most part high-class works, tending to the honor of God, the salvation of souls, and the civilisation of the people.*" How soon, alas, was this to change! Even while these words were written, the evil was already striking root, and steps had been taken by the civil as well as by the ecclesiastical power, to prevent the printing and spreading of noxious books.

But it was not until the beginning of the so-called Reformation that the boundless increase of heretical and other pernicious literature called for radical and extensive measures. They began in 1520 with the solemn condemnation of Luther's doctrine and the prohibition of his writings. About that time the first indexes or catalogues of forbidden books appeared. They were not issued by the popes, but emanated mostly from bishops, provincial councils, or universities. The civil power was expected to enforce them. In some cases the princes themselves or the magistrates of cities and republics issued their own indexes, in full harmony and after consultation with the clergy.

As the object of these measures was to safeguard the faithful against imminent danger, we can easily understand that catalogues of forbidden books were most numerous in those countries that were most exposed to heresy, namely, Germany, Belgium, France, and Northern Italy.

It is remarkable that Henry VIII of England, who afterwards fell away from the Church, was among the first to legislate against heretical books, his index of forbidden books appearing as early as 1526. After his apostasy he continued with increased severity the policy of prohibiting books which he deemed objectionable.

4. The Roman Index

More than thirty years after the first index of Henry VIII had appeared, the first Roman Index of Forbidden Books was compiled and issued by order of Paul IV. It remained in force only a few years, till 1564, when the so-called Tridentine Index was published under Pius IV. It was called "Tridentine," because it had been drawn up by a commission appointed for this purpose by the Council of Trent. It was milder than the Index of Paul IV, and contained divers "Index rules," the forerunners of the general decrees embodied in the Constitution "Officiorum ac munerum."

The Tridentine Index remained *the* Roman Index for more than three hundred years. Its "rules" were occasionally modified, new regulations were added or old ones abrogated, other books were inserted in the catalogue; but the essential features remained the same.

In 1897, Leo XIII took the matter up again. The index of forbidden books was thoroughly revised. About a thousand were dropped. The "rules," too, were overhauled, "to make them milder, without altering their nature, so that it cannot be difficult or irksome for any person of good will to obey them."

This, then, represents the whole book legislation of the Church. There are no other documents, except the decrees by which, as occasion demanded, individual books were forbidden. The encyclical of Pius X on Modernism merely enjoins on the bishops special vigilance in regard to publications infected with modernistic views.

This universal legislation, however, does not preclude the local prohibition of books by bishops or other ecclesiastical authorities. Thus Spain had, until 1820, its own Index, controlled by the Spanish Inquisition.

5. Books Forbidden by General or Particular Decrees

As we have already mentioned, the Constitution "Officiorum ac munerum" establishes the general laws by which books are forbidden. As will be seen in our Summary, these laws deal with classes of books. The only one named expressly is the Bible. But all the books clearly contained in these classes are as strictly, and sometimes even more strictly, condemned than those listed singly in the second part of the Index.

Pope Leo changed the Tridentine rules "without altering their nature." It is, indeed, difficult to see how the nature of these regulations could have been changed. They simply express the point of view from which the Church must look upon objectionable publications. While opposing and condemning spoken error, the Church surely cannot allow full sway to the printed. In regard to the second part, or Index proper, many wrong notions are current. One of these is, that this Index contains *all* the books forbidden by the Church, and that there are no others which we are obliged to avoid. From the foregoing remarks, it must, on the contrary, be concluded that there are many other books forbidden by the laws of the Church. The worst of them are not in this special Index at all, because they fall under the general decrees.

It is by no means the intention of the Roman authorities to catalogue all the literary virus that has been vomited forth by printing presses all over the world in the course of four and a half centuries. By means of the general laws laid down in the "Officiorum ac munerum" we are in all cases able to see our duty.

There are especially two purposes for which books are prohibited separately and by name.

Whenever there is a doubt about the nature of a book, recourse may be had to Rome; sometimes the Roman authorities appointed for this purpose, will take up the matter without being appealed to. They will investigate and decide by putting the book on the Index, or, by dismissing it. This is the case with most books publicly censured. It was the case with the books of Schell and Loisy, which, it was strongly urged by learned men, propagated ideas contrary, or at least dangerous, to the faith, though a host of followers admired them as orthodox masterpieces. Rome had to speak, and settled the controversy by condemning the books in question.

Dismissal does not always mean that a book is unobjectionable. The authorities may refrain from pronouncing deserved condemnation for reasons of prudence and expediency.

Sometimes the preservation of discipline or religious unity necessitates this step. Thus about two hundred years ago the Pope had imposed silence on two factions that were carrying on a theological feud. This silence was violated on both sides, a book appearing for the defence of either position. What was more natural than that both books should be put on the Index? These and similar cases could not be covered so clearly by the general decrees.

What has thus far been said, offers a partial solution of another current error. The Index is not a studiously selected, not even a systematically arranged catalogue of objectionable books. It was the need of the moment, doctrinal blunders, cavillations and heresies, grievous trespasses against discipline and charity, proceeding from animosity or want of tact, that caused the insertion of most of the books. In nearly all cases the Roman authorities confine themselves to books concerning which they are appealed to; and as there is no system in the making of these appeals, there can be no system in the condemnations. In the new Leonine edition of the Index the books are enumerated alphabetically by authors or pseudonyms; anonymous books are listed according to titles.

It must now be obvious to the attentive reader why most of the books put on the Index are works on theology, or on the history and government of the Church, and why (as may be expected in the case of such publications), a considerable percentage are written in Latin. However, a goodly number of books are on the Index because they are detrimental to good morals. There are very few there which treat of the natural sciences. The Index will not busy itself with publications on electricity or X-rays, unless an author on a subject of this sort devote a considerable part of his work to attacks upon religion.

There are some well-meaning people who, while agreeing that the productions of Zola, Dumas and other writers of the same sort, fully deserve condemnation, cannot understand why works like Ranke's History of the Popes, which is an acknowledged authority in its line, should be proscribed. Such works are not on the Index for the good things they contain, but for the poison they mix with the wholesome food so cleverly that it takes more than ordinary scholarship and discretion to separate the one from the other.

The Roman Committee of Cardinals, which has charge of this part of ecclesiastical discipline, is not at all bent on proscribing books. Works like the one mentioned are never put on the Index unless it is quite clear that the mischief to be feared from them will far outweigh the good they may do. Scholars and students well grounded in their faith, who have a real and legitimate cause for reading a forbidden book can easily obtain a dispensation.

It is clear from the preceding explanations that a book may sometimes be dropped from the Index. This is done when a book has long ceased to be dangerous, or a cause of dissension, or if it has fallen into oblivion. Thus Pope Leo XIII caused to be expunged about a thousand titles. This does not imply a reproach for the authorities of former centuries, much less the giving up of an iota of the old principles.

6. Duties Imposed by Law and by Nature

Suppose a person were so well grounded in faith and virtue, so thoroughly versed in theology, philosophy, and the natural sciences, that the reading of books e. g. on Christian Science, or the works of Voltaire, would not harm him. The Index prohibits these books; would he whom they could not harm be allowed to read them? As we put the case, he would, by reading them, not commit the sin of seriously endangering his soul. Yet he would sin by disregarding a positive law of the Church. These laws are like the precautionary measures taken by the civil authorities in times of epidemic; if they are to have the desired effect, they must be observed by all. When the community is under quarantine, those who declare themselves free from the disease must observe the regulations as well as the rest.

Let those who think they have *a good reason* for reading a forbidden book, and who are not mistaken in supposing that there is no danger for them, humbly ask for permission, as did the Saints. By doing so they declare that the standpoint of the Church is theirs, and that they willingly submit to a power which was entrusted with the care of "teaching to observe whatsoever I have commanded you." "We have to develop a loving habit of loyalty and obedience to the Church as to Christ, our Savior."

Suppose, on the other hand, there were no Church laws prohibiting pernicious reading. In that case should we be allowed to read any book we pleased? By no means. We should then, it is true, by reading, e. g., Zola's novels, not commit an act of disobedience to the Church. But, as already hinted, there is another duty imposed on us by God Himself—the grave duty to guard our soul from serious danger. This duty does not depend on any positive law or decree of authority, and it equally binds the Christian and the non-Christian. It is expressed in the fifth commandment: "Thou shalt not kill." This duty corresponds on our part to what we ask of God in the sixth petition of the Our Father: "Lead us not into temptation." We should undoubtedly violate it by reading Zola's filthy works. The prohibition of these works by the Church merely adds another obligation to that imposed by the natural law, thereby considerably strengthening our will and enabling us to resist every enticement to read what can be read only at a serious risk to our soul.

This grave duty, therefore, is not imposed by the Church and cannot be taken away by the Church. It is a natural duty and as such remains in force even after we are granted a formal permission, which is neither intended nor able to suppress temptations that may arise from the perusal of bad books. If we have a good reason to apply for permission—curiosity is not a good reason—then and then only can we expect a special protection from Divine Providence. Of course, this protection does not dispense us from the necessity of using all the means of self-protection, both natural and supernatural.

I know of a priest who was in every way a model man. He fell suddenly away from the Church, married, and is now a foremost champion in the ranks of the enemy. His apostasy is, not without reason, attributed to the reading of infidel books, though no doubt he had the necessary dispensation. There was another priest, who has meanwhile died the death of the just, a celebrated author and art critic. In writing a work on Voltaire he had to study the books of that arch-agnostic. He obtained the requisite permission, but, while perusing Voltaire's writings, he was on his knees, to implore, as it were, by this humble posture the protection of God against the wicked influence to which he was exposed.

St. Francis of Sales, the great and learned Bishop of Geneva, had obtained permission to read the books of heretics in order to refute them, and he is careful to let his readers know the fact, at the same time thanking God in pathetic words that his soul had suffered no harm in so great a danger.

This grave natural duty in the choice of our reading matter extends much farther than the legislation of the Church. Parents and priests do not comply with their obligation of controlling the reading of their charges if they merely look up the Index to see whether a certain book is mentioned there. If an otherwise unobjectionable book contains an obscene passage of a page or so, no one will claim that it falls under the general law prohibiting obscene books. Nor is it likely to be put on the Index. Yet such a book is apt to work havoc in the innocent soul of your daughter or son, perhaps in your own. As long as that passage is in it, the book—even though it is not on the Index—cannot and must not, under pain of sin, be allowed in the hands of children.

Would that this twofold duty were always faithfully complied with, especially in our large cities, where books of every sort are within easy reach. Do not many, perhaps all, public libraries offer among other books such as are "derogatory to the Church, the hierarchy, the religious state," and especially novels which "defend as lawful or tolerable, freemasonry, suicide, divorce"? How can we expect our young people to have Catholic views on courtship and marriage, on the priesthood, on the veneration of the saints, if we allow them to imbibe the ideas of such writers as Balzac or Dumas? It is deplorable enough that the modern novel is the catechism of millions outside of the Church. We must not allow it to displace the Catholic catechism or to unteach, totally or in part, the truths taught by it.

7. Who Puts Books On The Index?

The popes have at all times exercised the prerogative of their supreme office as guardians of the faith by condemning books opposed to the faith. The latest of such condemnations is that, in 1862, of the works of the Munich professor, Frohschammer, who answered this condemnation by falling away from the Church. There are in all 144 books that were individually proscribed by a papal document. In Pope Leo's edition they are marked with a dagger. Yet only in cases of the utmost importance did the popes act themselves. To facilitate the government of the world-wide Church, in the course of centuries special committees of cardinals were appointed, to whom part of the pontiff's various duties were entrusted. These committees are styled Congregations. A larger or smaller number of learned priests and bishops, generally called Consultors, assist the cardinals and practically do the greater part of the work, though the final decision in all cases is reserved to the cardinals.

The highest of these Roman Congregations is the *Sacrum Officium* or "General Inquisition," called also the "Congregation of the Holy Office," of which the Pope himself is Prefect. Its purpose is especially to watch over the purity of faith. It is this august body that, after the Pope himself, is in the first place called to judge the doctrines propounded in any book. It was this Congregation that performed the preparatory work for the first Index of Paul IV, and, although another congregation for the examining of books was soon after established, the *Sacrum Officium* continued to exercise the same power. As may be expected, especially such works as seemed to affect the integrity of the faith, were submitted to this supreme court. In our days the works of the French priest Loisy were proscribed by the *Sacrum Officium.*

But the bulk of this work is at present performed by the *Congregatio Indicis librorum prohibitorum,* or "Congregation of the Index of Forbidden Books." It was founded by Saint Pius V in 1571, seven years after the publication of the Tridentine Index. Since then about eighty per cent. of all individual prohibitions of books have emanated from it. Its Prefect is a cardinal. The present one is Cardinal Segna. The perpetual assistant and secretary are always members of the Dominican order. Besides the seven or ten cardinals there are about thirty consultors, many of whom are bishops.

Though three or four prohibitions of books have emanated from other Roman authorities, the practice has been to let either the

Sacrum Officium or the Congregation of the Index decide in all cases. The latter Congregation, moreover, had to register all condemnations pronounced by any of the legitimate authorities and to see that they were entered in the new editions of the Index.

Our present Holy Father, Pius X, has lately brought about a long desired reform in the central government of the Church. The competency of many of the Roman Congregations has been more clearly defined, and several of those originally instituted have been either suppressed or united with others. The Congregation of the Index has received a wider sphere and greater power. While formerly it passed only on books in regard to which it was expressly appealed to, it has now become a regular vigilance committee for the whole Church. The Holy Father says: "For the future it shall be the province of this Sacred Congregation not only to examine diligently the books reported to it, to prohibit them, if this should seem well, and to concede dispensations; but also to officially investigate in the best available way whether writings of any kind that should be condemned are being circulated; and to remind the ordinaries how strictly they are bound to condemn pernicious writings and to denounce them to the Holy See."

On the relation of the Congregation of the Index to that of the *Sacrum Officium* (Holy Office) the Pope says: "As the prohibition of books has very frequently the scope of defense of the Faith, which is also the object of the Congregation of the Holy Office, we decree that in future in all things relating to the prohibition of books, and in those alone, the Cardinals, Consultors and officers of both congregations, may communicate with one another, and that all of them shall be bound by the same secret."

The Roman Congregations are not infallible. But they represent the Pope in his highest capacity as shepherd of the entire flock of Christ. Therefore we owe them obedience. Their regulations and orders must find us even more willing to obey than those of our bishops and pastors, to whom only a small portion of Christ's kingdom is entrusted.

8. The Method of Examination

Our confidence in the fairness of the verdicts of the S. Congregation of the Index will be much increased, if we acquaint ourselves with the method it follows in carrying out its arduous, odious and yet very important task. This method is practically the same for both the Holy Office and the Index. The usual procedure is based mainly on the regulations laid down in the Bull of Pope Benedict XIV, "Sollicita ac provida."

When a book is reported to the Index Congregation, the secretary first tries to ascertain whether it is worth examining. He also inquires by letter from bishops and other reliable persons about the advisability of a condemnation. Several consultors assist him in this preliminary investigation; but the Cardinal Prefect has to ratify their decision.

If they think the book should be examined, it is handed to a consultor, who has to study it carefully and to draw up a detailed report, noting exactly the passages which he finds objectionable, and conscientiously pointing out all redeeming features. His report together with the book is passed on to other consultors, each of whom can thus satisfy himself whether the first "examiner's" verdict is fair, and has also an opportunity to formulate his own view. One question they have to answer is, whether the condemnation is likely to have a good effect.

After comparing the opinions of the consultors, the secretary of the Congregation draws up an official statement of the reasons for and against a prohibition, which statement together with the book is submitted to the Cardinal Prefect, by whose orders it is printed and a copy sent to each cardinal and consultor of the Congregation.

Next a preparatory meeting of the consultors is called for a previous discussion. The consultor who examined the book speaks first, then all the others, beginning with the youngest. The secretary carefully records the views of each consultor, together with his reasons.

At least ten days must elapse between this meeting and the solemn session of the whole Congregation, in which the question is finally decided by a vote of the cardinals.

The decision arrived at is commonly given in one of these four technical phrases: *Damnetur*, "condemned"; *dimittatur*, "dismissed"; *donec corrigatur*, "forbidden until amended"; *res dilata*, "the case is postponed." The verdict *donec corrigatur* of course, can only be given when a book admits of correction; when it is thoroughly bad (e. g. written for the sole purpose of eulogizing Freemasonry or maligning Catholic bishops), a *donec corrigatur* would have no meaning.

Finally, the secretary of the Congregation lays the whole matter before the Pope, who, if he sees fit, authorizes the publication of the decree.

Nobody will deny that this is a very excellent method of procedure. Under it a book is examined at least three times, and twenty-five or thirty picked scholars participate in the proceedings, each of whom has taken a solemn oath never to allow himself to be influenced by sympathy or antipathy and to have nothing in view but the eternal welfare of souls.

If the author is a Catholic, he must be informed before the decree is published. If but a few copies of the book have been sold, and the author promises either to suppress it, or to issue an amended edition, if possible, the decree is not published. But even when this cannot be prevented, e. g. when a whole edition is already in circulation, credit is given to the author in the decree itself for declaring his submission, by adding the words: *auctor laudabiliter se subjecit*, "the author has praiseworthily submitted."

Great care is taken to have all books examined by men who are not only well versed in the subject matter, but who also understand thoroughly the language in which they happen to be written. Nor does the Congregation in important cases confine itself to its regular consultors; whenever it seems advisable, the services of other competent critics are enlisted.

All the members of the Congregation are bound by oath to keep absolute secrecy with regard to every detail of the official transactions, no matter whether a book under discussion is finally condemned or not. By this means each feels more free in giving his opinion, and the reputation of the author is spared as long and as much as possible.

9. The Spirit of the Congregation of the Index

As to the spirit that should actuate the members of the Congregation of the Index, the rules laid down for its consultors by Benedict XIV in the Bull "Sollicita ac provida" are instructive.

"*Ipsos … monemus ac vehementer hortamur ut in examine iudicioque librorum sequentes regulas diligenter inspiciant accurateque custodiant.*" "We wish to admonish and exhort them most urgently to study carefully and observe accurately the following rules for examining and judging books:

1. Let them not imagine that it is their duty to use every means to bring about the condemnation of the books submitted to them. They ought rather to study such books conscientiously, without passion or anxiety (sedato animo), in order to furnish such well-found observations, such objective reasons, as will enable the Congregation to pass a just verdict.

2. Should a consultor find that he is not competent to judge a book which he is asked to examine, let him know that he will not be free from guilt, either before God or man, unless he at once confesses his incompetence. Far from damaging his reputation with the pope or the cardinals, such an avowal will rather gain their esteem and praise for his straightforwardness and honesty.

3. Let them set aside absolutely all prejudice in favor of nation, family, school or order; let them relinquish all party spirit, and keep before their minds the undoubted doctrine of the Church, as laid down in the decrees of the councils, in papal documents, etc., knowing that there are opinions that, while they seem certain to one nation, school, or order, are, with the knowledge of the Holy See, opposed by others; the Holy See leaving all these opinions in their degree of probability.

4. It must also be borne in mind that it is impossible to judge fairly the meaning of a passage, unless the entire book is studied, and unless the various statements found in different sections are compared with one another, and the whole purpose of the book is steadily kept in view.

5. If an author who enjoys the reputation of sound theological learning, has used expressions which might be understood in a wrong as well as in a right meaning, fairness demands that they be, as far as possible, interpreted in his favor.

These and similar rules ... must be kept before the minds of the consultors, in order that they may have due regard for their own conscience, the good name of authors, the interests of the Church, and the welfare of souls."

10. Further Explanations

A. Why an Author is Not Permitted to Defend His Book

If an author could accompany every copy of his work that leaves the bookstore or library, he would be able to explain obscure passages and to show what meaning he wished doubtful phrases to convey to the reader. It is precisely because he cannot multiply himself that he employs printer's ink to convey his ideas to others. It must, therefore, be supposed that his words mean what he intends to say. The reader, at any rate, has no corrective. He has only the book, not the author to fall back upon. It is impossible to recur to the author when there is question of the correctness or incorrectness of a book. If the author has to be called upon to explain the meaning of his book, he should have left it unprinted.

Moreover, it is hardly credible, as Pope Benedict XIV points out, that anything an author might advance in his favor, should escape so many examiners without receiving due attention and emphasis.

The whole procedure is primarily not intended as a measure against the author, although pecuniary loss *may* ensue, but to protect the faithful. A condemnation is rather a warning to the would-be reader, than a punishment inflicted upon the author. It is not an act of jurisdiction. Were the author's personal views under investigation, he would be summoned personally before another tribunal and tried according to a method that would give him the amplest opportunity to defend himself.

These considerations also show that the condemnation of a book after its author's death is not unreasonable. A book remains what it is independently of its author. Nor would it change the nature of a book were the author afterwards to prove his orthodoxy to the satisfaction of the authorities, or to do penance in sackcloth and ashes, or for the rest of his mortal life consort with the Trappists.

Were it morally certain, however, that almost all the copies of a book were destroyed, a prohibitory decree would fail of its purpose.

B. The Index Does Not Advertise Bad Books

Now and then there is expressed an apprehension lest the Index, far from suppressing, rather advertises bad books and arouses a desire to read them. It is even maintained that in some cases evil-minded authors have intentionally written so as to get their books put on the Index.

Now, every prohibitory law may have the effect of increasing the inclination of men towards the prohibited thing or act. Thus a person may possibly feel a stronger appetite for meat on Friday than on any other day of the week. We have inherited this tendency from

Eve, who, when tempted, saw that the forbidden fruit *"was good to eat and fair to the eye and delightful to behold,"* and then proceeded to violate the first prohibitory law ever given. But is that a reason to do away with every prohibitory law?

Who does not see at once that the Index must prove a very poor advertising medium? Those who have it are certainly not the prospective buyers of immoral novels or of works which propagate heretical views in theology; while those who hanker after sensationalism or doubtful theology will not invest $2.25 for a book list which contains, e. g. for the year 1898, fully eight titles, four of which are German, and for 1903 fifteen, all French.

This side of the question, as we have remarked elsewhere, is also in each case carefully weighed by the Sacred Congregation, before it resolves upon a prohibition.

Even if the sale of a book should be increased by the fact of its condemnation, the Index would nevertheless achieve its main purpose, namely, to warn the faithful that the ideas advocated in the proscribed book are contrary to faith and morals. This is enough for all men of good will to enable them to shun the poison. Those who refuse to heed the warning will have to blame their own ignorance or malice if the reading of a condemned book results in spiritual hurt.

C. Index Decisions Not Omitted for Fear of Apostasies

A book, we are reminded, often represents the opinions not only of its author, but of many of his disciples and admirers. By forbidding it and thus branding such opinions as erroneous, it is said, many influential men may become embittered and may even be driven into an attitude of open hostility.

However, the Church is in duty bound to exercise her guardianship; which she cannot do if every one is to have his own way. Nor can the Church neglect the mass of her children in order to accommodate this or that coterie or school, whose opinions are manifestly wrong.

Moreover, to be a trustworthy guide, the Church must state the truth clearly and unmistakably. The faithful are not guided by ambiguous circumlocutions, by terms that may be understood in two or perhaps more ways. Neither may she keep exclusively in the lofty heights of theory; but she must instruct with regard to the facts of everyday life. The dangers arising from books are *concrete* not *abstract*, and they must be met by concrete measures. This can be done effectively only by an energetic and unmistakable "thou shalt not," which makes men realize that they are "under authority."

No one has ever stated the truth more clearly, more unmistakably than Christ our Lord. Was it not precisely for this very fact that "many of His disciples went back and walked no more with Him"? (John 6, 67.)

D. The "Good Catholic."

"I am a Catholic. I live up to my religion and go regularly to the sacraments. I have had a good Catholic education and hear a sermon every Sunday. I do not see why I should be afraid to read any book, even if it belonged to those forbidden by the Index."

You may do so; but you may fare in consequence as David fared—David who was a saint and yet committed adultery and murder. If you read a forbidden book without permission, you are as good a Catholic as one who eats meat on Friday. The object of the law of abstinence is to make sure that every Christian performs at least a certain minimum of penance. Now there are saintly persons who, in imitation of our crucified Savior, do more penance on ordinary days than the average Catholic does by abstaining from meat on twenty or more Fridays; and yet they are not exempted from the law of abstinence and would be the last to claim such an exemption.

Similarly the object of the Index is to make sure that every Christian avoids at least the worst books. By obeying its laws we declare that our standpoint is that of the Church of God. This result cannot be obtained unless the prohibition is made universal, exempting no one, no matter how pious or learned he may be. Therefore, *all* Christians, good and bad, priests, religious and lay people, students and professors, unless they have a dispensation, are bound by the ecclesiastical laws regarding books. By asking for a dispensation we implicitly acknowledge and approve of the official position of the Church on the subject of wicked books, and, so far as in us lies, ratify and sanction the reasons which lead to their condemnation.

You say you are a good Catholic, and therefore this law does not bind you. Are there any commandments of the Church that bind only bad Catholics?

E. A Mortal Sin

"I am told that a transgression of the Index law is a mortal sin. Can it be true that the Church, the kindest of mothers, should load us down with such a severe obligation?"

According to the theologians, the reading of a forbidden book, or of a considerable part of it, *is* a mortal sin. The selection of the books on which our souls feed is a matter of no small importance. True, the Church is the kindest of mothers; but she is also the wisest. To direct the consciences of her children and "*to restrain them from the reading of bad books as from a deadly poison,*" is the great object of her legislation. Under the leadership of a mastermind like that of Leo XIII, the Roman authorities have labored for years in formulating the present ecclesiastical laws about books. These laws are the voice of the supreme pastor, the successor of St. Peter. Let us not spurn it like the heathen and the publican.

F. The Galileo Case

The Roman Congregations are no more infallible than our bishops and pastors. And yet there is practically but one case, during more than three centuries, in which they are accused of having made a mistake. It is the condemnation, by both the Holy Office and the Index, of *Galileo Galilei Linceo* (died 1639) for defending the theory that the earth moves around its own axis and around the sun.

This teaching was according to the common belief of Catholics and Protestants, at that time, clearly opposed to Holy Scripture, which the Church was bound to vindicate. If Galileo's theory was true, the traditional interpretation of sundry Bible texts would have had to be abandoned.

The Church had weighty reasons for not allowing this. The new theory was not at all certain. Galileo himself admitted he could not establish more than a probability. Several very obvious objections he was unable to explain satisfactorily. None of the real proofs used in our days were known to him. He was told by the Jesuit Cardinal Bellarmin, if he could advance any convincing proof for his theory, the traditional interpretation of those passages would be given up. But all Galileo had to offer was an ingenious hypothesis. Had he advocated it as such with due respect for the time-honored interpretation of the Book of Books, had he not used bold, sometimes bitter and defying language, no steps would have been taken against him, who had until then been a favorite of the pope and of many dignitaries. As matters stood, "the Church could wait for the education of a physical system, but she could not allow a change in the universally accepted interpretation of Scripture, before the necessity of such a change was proved." (Guggenberger, History of the Christian Era. Vol. II, pp. 456, etc.)

"The marvelous unanimity of the enemies of the Church in concentrating all their attacks against the Roman Congregation on the case of Galileo, is a striking negative testimony to the value of the decisions of courts which have been at work for centuries." (*Rome.*)

G. State and Protestant Book Laws

As we have already remarked, Henry VIII continued his policy of proscribing books opposed to his views long after he had constituted himself the head of the English Church. Between 1526 and 1546 there were issued by the King's authority nine catalogues of books which Englishmen were forbidden to read. Among these books were the works of the continental "reformers"; for some years the English Bible; also writings against the King's matrimonial projects.

The Protestants on the continent followed the same system. Calvin condemned a Spanish physician, who happened to come to Geneva, to be burned at the stake, because he had written a heretical book. The Protestant princes and republics had each its special book-legislation, which was made to serve not only religious but also political purposes.

After the middle of the eighteenth century, in almost all Catholic countries, the civil power usurped the monopoly of proscribing books, and practiced it in a truly despotic way. Thus in Austria 639 books were forbidden within five years. No book was allowed to be printed without *previous* permission, not even on forestry or cattle-raising. Bishops were severely reproved for enforcing the prohibitions of the Roman Index in their seminaries.

Napoleon I had a publisher shot, practically without trial, for issuing a work contrary to his political plans. One book was publicly burned because it contained the picture of Pius VII. To enable the authorities to control the book trade more effectively, no printing establishment was allowed to have, in Paris more than four, and in the provinces more than two, presses.

Needless to remark, the civil authorities *have* the right to prohibit books that seriously endanger the common welfare. If they use this right in a reasonable way, their measures are likely to bring about good and prevent evil. We all have occasional opportunities to observe this in the measures taken against immoral literature by the police or the post-office department.

H. Some Examples of Submission to the Index

The first Roman Index, that of 1559, was considered rather severe. One of the influential men who tried hard to have its provisions softened, was *Blessed Peter Canisius*, the "Second Apostle of Germany." Yet the very letters he wrote to Rome for this purpose show that he scrupulously observed all the regulations, though he himself, called the "Hammer of Heretics," surely incurred little personal risk by reading forbidden books.

About 1698, a book by *Archbishop Fénelon* was under investigation at Rome. Fénelon was a great scholar and one of the greatest preachers of all centuries, but he was also a loyal son of the Church. He knew a condemnation of his book would mean his own condemnation in the eyes of Catholic France. His friends as well as his antagonists were eagerly awaiting Rome's decision on one of the great churchman's books. At last the verdict was pronounced in the most solemn way by the Pope himself, and it was a condemnation. Fénelon was just ascending his pulpit, March 25, 1699, when his brother broke the news to him. The great Archbishop at once proceeded to read to his own flock the papal document and preached an eloquent sermon on the obedience every Christian owes to his superiors. We can imagine what a profound impression his words must have made. His was a truly heroic example of self-abnegation.

In 1861 there died in Munich *Ernest von Lasaulx*, a famous professor of the University. In his writings he had now and then been very bold, and it was rumored that the Congregation of the Index thought of censuring some of his books. Von Lasaulx knew this. A few weeks before his death he made an implicit retraction of the errors he might have involuntarily committed, which was forwarded to Rome by his friends. Already some years before he had declared that he had never intended to contravene the doctrine of the Church, but that he feared there were many errors in his books. "If Rome would think it advisable to put my books on the Index, I should consider the verdict perfectly just, *since I firmly believe that such measures are truly in the interest of the Catholic Church in our times.*" Four of his

books were really condemned after his death.

In July, 1906, an Italian novel, Il Santo, (The Saint) by Fogazzaro, was

put on the Index. The author "submitted himself." An American

edition of the book had meanwhile appeared; "but the prohibition

by the Roman authorities was duly respected by the publishers of

the leading Catholic papers of America, which declined to accept

advertisements of the book." (Putnam.)

SECTION II
A SUMMARY OF THE INDEX

1. Our Duties in Relation to Forbidden Books

Rule 1. We are not allowed to read forbidden books, nor any

considerable portion of them, even if those portions be in

themselves harmless. If, however, a book is forbidden merely on account of the one or other objectionable passage it contains, the objection ceases as soon as these passages are expunged or rendered illegible.

Rule 2. No one, whether he be the owner or not, is allowed to keep a forbidden book. He must either destroy it, or give or sell it to some one who has permission, or he must obtain permission for himself.

Rule 3. It is not lawful for a Catholic publisher or printer to issue, or print, or reprint forbidden books. Nor may a bookseller keep such books in stock, unless he has obtained formal leave to do so.

Note 1. Although all the members of a Catholic family should endeavor to keep forbidden books out of the home, the head of the household is chiefly responsible before God. It is to be remarked, however, that Catholic librarians or servants do not violate this law by keeping, handling, or cataloguing forbidden books for their employers, e. g. in the latter's house, or in a public library.

Note 2. If a book or any particular issue of a forbidden periodical calls for a speedy public refutation, *and* if permission to peruse it cannot be waited for, any educated Catholic, who may be reasonably presumed to be competent to refute it by sermon, lecture or newspaper article, may read such book or periodical without awaiting special permission.

Note 3. In all other cases, each and every Catholic, be he priest or layman, professor or student, must first obtain permission. Neither piety, nor learning, nor position exempts one from this law. The permission is granted by bishops and their vicars general, who can also delegate this power to others. When asking for this permission the applicant should mention the book which he thinks he has good reasons to read.

The juridical question, whether the bishop's faculty is *ordinaria,* or *quasi-ordinaria,* or *extra-ordinaria,* and how far it extends, is not within the scope of this Summary.

Note 4. All who are dispensed from the Church law regarding forbidden books, must apply every possible precaution, in order that they may not suffer injury to their faith or purity of heart. Such precautions are: the hearing of sermons, the reading of Catholic books, the frequenting of Catholic society, regular prayers, and the frequent and humble reception of the sacraments.

2. Forbidden Books

Rule 4. General Rule.—Translations of a forbidden book into any language, if they faithfully reproduce the original, are also forbidden.

A. The General Decrees Prohibit the Following Publications

Rule 5, a. Books defending heresies, i. e. doctrines contrary to divine revelation.

b. Books derogatory to God, the Blessed Virgin, the Saints.

c. Books vilifying the sacraments, the clerical or religious state, the hierarchy, the Church.

Rule 6. Books professedly treating of, narrating or teaching lewdness and obscenity.

Rule 7. Books teaching or recommending sorcery, Spiritism, Christian Science, or other superstitions.

Rule 8. Books defending as lawful or harmless Freemasonry, divorce, Socialism, suicide, duelling.

Rule 9. *Those newspapers and periodicals* which, not only now and then, but regularly and of set purpose, attack religion or morality, or propagate anti-Catholic views.

Rule 10. Episcopal approbation, to be printed in the beginning or at the end of the book, is required for all editions of the Bible or parts of the Bible in any language, likewise for all prayer books, books of devotion and of practical piety. Without episcopal authorization such publications are forbidden, though they may have been issued by the most learned and pious men.

Note 1. Leaflets which are so small that they cannot be called books, or even booklets or pamphlets, do not fall under this law. But if they are not approved by the bishop, the duty of making sure that they contain nothing erroneous devolves upon those who use them.

Summaries of indulgences, however, no matter how small, always need episcopal approbation and may not be circulated without it.

Note 2. All editions of the Bible, edited by non-Catholics, in ancient as well as modern languages, are permitted to those, and those only, who are engaged in serious theological or biblical studies, provided, however, that the PROLEGOMENA AND ANNOTATIONS do not of set purpose impugn the Catholic faith. It is not enough that the text itself is faithfully and completely rendered.

Note 3. An exception has also been made in favor of those classics, ancient and modern, which on account of their obscenity fall under rule 6. In as far as they are models of style they may be read by persons engaged in teaching university or higher college classes of literature, by those who are preparing for such a position in the near future, and by those who, on account of their profession, e. g. as critics or authors of literary works, cannot well do without them. (See note 4 above.)

Whenever we know, or discover while reading, that a book undoubtedly belongs to any one of these classes, we may be sure that it is a work which our Holy Mother the Church does not wish to see in our hands, and we must then act according to the words of Christ: "He who heareth you, heareth Me, and he who despiseth you despiseth Me." No need of first looking up the catalogue of forbidden books; whether the volume in question is mentioned there or not, makes no difference. Nor does it matter what the literary character of the book is. An apparently learned history of the seizure of Rome in 1870, written with the obvious intention of maligning Pius IX, is forbidden just as well as a novel written for the same purpose, or the prayer book of some Protestant sect.

B. Books Forbidden by Particular Decrees

The following list contains a number of titles which every English-speaking Catholic ought to know. All the books that have been put on the Index during the last few years have been mentioned, not so much for completeness' sake, as because they contain the palmary error of our time, namely: Modernism, and among its doctrines especially the unchristian treatment of the Bible. None of these books are written in English. But some have been and others may soon be translated. Their titles, as well as those of most other foreign books, are given in English.

- *Addison, Jos.*

  - Remarks on Several Parts of Italy.

- *Bacon, Francis.*

  - De   dignitate   et   augmentis   scientiarum. (On the Dignity and Increase of Science.)

- *Balzac, Honoré de.*

    - All novels.

- *Bentham, Jeremy.*

    - Three Tracts, etc.

    - Deontology or the Science of Morality.

- *Bingham, Jos.*

    - Origines Ecclesiasticæ, or The Antiquities of the Christian Church.

- *Blunt, John James.*

    - Vestiges of Ancient Manners and Customs, etc.

- *Bois, Jules.*

- Satanism.

- *Bruno, Giordano.*

  - The Conflict of Religion, Morals and Science in Contemporary Education.

-

Bunsen, Christian Chas. J.

  - Hippolytus and His Age, or The Doctrine and Practice of the Church of Rome under Commodus and Alexander Severus, etc.

- *Bureau, Paul.*

  - The Moral Crisis in Modern Times. Preface by M. Alfred Croiset.

- *Burgess, Richard.*

  - Lectures on the Insufficiency of Unrevealed Religion.

- *Cudworth, Ralph.*

  - The True Intellectual System of the Universe, etc.

- *Darwin, Erasmus.*

  - Zoönomia or the Laws of Organic Life.

- *Denis, Chas.*

  - An Apologetic Lenten Course on the Fundamental Dogmas, 1903.

  - Church and State: The Lessons of the Present Hour, 1903.

- *Descartes, René.*

- Meditations on Original Philosophy.

- *Dimnet, Ernest.*

    - Catholic Thought in England.

-

    Döllinger, John Joseph Ignatius.

    - The Pope and the Council.

    - Janus.

- *Draper, John William.*

    - History of the Conflicts Between Religion and Science.

- *Duggan, James.*

    - Steps towards Reunion.

- *Dumas, Alexander* (father and son).

    - All novels, except The Count of Monte-cristo.

- *Earle, John Chas.*

    - The Spiritual Body.

    - The Forty Days, or Christ Between His Resurrection and Ascension.

- *Fénelon, François de Salignac.*

    - The Principles of the Saints.

- *Ferrière, Émile.*

    - The Soul a Function of the Brain.

    - The Apostles.

- Darwinism.

- The Scientific Blunders of the Bible.

- Matter and Energy.

- Paganism of the Hebrews.

- Life and Soul.

- The Myths of the Bible.

-

Ffoulkes, Edmund S.

- Christendom's Divisions.

- The Church's Creed or the Crown's Creed.

- *Fogazzaro, Antonio.*

- The Saint (a novel).

- *Frohschammer, Jacob.*

    - Origin of the Human Soul.

    - Introduction to Philosophy.

    - On the Liberty of Science.

    - Christianity and Modern Science.

    - The Right of One's Own Conviction.

    - The New Knowledge and the New Faith.

- *Georgel, Michél.*

    - Matter: Its Deification, Its Rehabilitation, and Its Ultimate

      Destiny.

- *Gibbon, Edward.*

    - History of the Decline and Fall of the Roman Empire.

- *Goblet d'Alviella, Eug.*

    - The Idea of God.

- *Goldsmith, Oliver.*

    - An Abridged History of England From the Invasion of

      Julius Cæsar to the Death of George II.

-

  Graf, Arthur.

    - The Devil.

- *Gregorovius, Ferdinand.*

- History of the City of Rome During the Middle Ages.

- The Sepulchral Monuments of the Popes.

- Urban VIII in Opposition to Spain and the Emperor.

- Athenaïs: The History of a Byzantine Empress.

- Wanderings in Italy (fifth volume), Scenes in Apulia.

- *Hallam, Henry.*

  - The Constitutional History of England, etc.

  - View of the State of Europe During the Middle Ages.

- *Heine, Heinrich.*

  - De l'Allemagne.

- De la France.

- Reisebilder.

- Neue Gedichte.

- *Hilaire de Paris.*

  - Exposition of the Rule of St. Francis.

- *Hobbes, Thomas.*

  - All works.

-

Houtin, Albert.

  - The Biblical Question among the Catholics of France in the XIX Century.

- The Biblical Question in the XX Century.

- My Troubles with My Bishop.

- Americanism.

- The Crisis of the Clergy.

- *Hugo, Victor.*

    - Notre Dame de Paris.

    - Les Misérables.

- *Hume, David.*

    - All works.

- *James I, King of England.*

    - Basilikon dōron (Royal Gift) divided into three books.

- Triplici nodo triplex cuneus, etc.

- Meditatio in Orationem dominicam.

- Meditatio in caput XXVII evangelii S. Matthali.

- *Kant, Immanuel.*

  - Critique of Pure Reason.

- *Laberthonnière, Lucien.*

  - Essays on Religious Philosophy.

  - Christian Realism and Grecian Idealism.

-

  Lacaze, Félix.

  - To Lourdes with Zola.

- *Lang, Andrew.*

    - Myth, Ritual and Religion.

- *Lasserre, Henri.*

    - The Holy Gospels.

- *Lefranc, E.* (pseudonym).

    - The Conflicts of Science and the Bible.

- *Le Morin, Jean.*

    - Truths of Yesterday?

- *Lenau, Nicolaus.*

    - Die Albigenser.

- *Lenormant, François.*

- The Beginnings of History.

- *LeRoy, Edouard.*

  - Dogma and Criticism.

- *Locke, John.*

  - An Essay Concerning Human Understanding.

  - The Reasonableness of Christianity, etc.

- *Loisy, Alfred.*

  - Gospel Studies.

  - The Gospel and the Church.

  - The Fourth Gospel.

  - Apropos of a Little Book.

- The Religion of Israel.

-

Maurice, Frederick D.

- Theological Essays.

- *Mill, John Stuart.*

  - Principles of Political Economy.

- *Milton, John.*

  - Literæ   pseudo-senatus   Anglicani,   Cromwellii

    reliquorumque perduellium nomine conscriptæ.

- *Mivart, St. George.*

  - Happiness in Hell.

- *Montesquieu, Chas. de Secondat de.*

    - The Spirit of the Laws.

    - Persian Letters.

- *Müller, Joseph.*

    - Reform Catholicism.

- *Negri, Ada.*

    - Fatalism.

- *Olive, Jos.*

    - Letters to the Members of the Pious and Devout Society of the Heart of Jesus, etc.

- *Osborne, Francis.*

- Miscellaneous Works.

- *Payot, Jules.*

  - About Faith.

  - Before Entering Life.

  -

    Program of Modernism (a reply to the encyclical).

- *Planchet, Franc. Regis.*

  - Episcopal Absolutism in the Mexican Republic.

- *Pufendorf, Samuel von.*

  - Introduction to the History of the Principal States of Europe.

- (Also four Latin works.)

- *Quiévreux, Camille.*

  - Paganism in the XIX Century.

- *Ranke, Leopold.*

  - The Roman Popes: Their Church and Their State in the XVI and XVII Centuries.

- *Renan, Ernest.*

  - Practically all his works (the Index names nineteen).

- *Renouf, Peter LePage.*

  - The Condemnation of Pope Honorius.

- *Richardson, Samuel.*

- Pamela, or Virtue Rewarded.

- *Robertson, Wm.*

  - The History of the Reign of the Emperor Charles V.

-

Rohling, August.

  - The Kingdom of the Future. (Der Zukunftsstaat.)

- *Roscoe, William.*

  - The Life and Pontificate of Leo X.

- *Rosmini-Serbati, Antonio.*

  - The Constitution according to Social Justice.

  - Of the Five Wounds of Holy Church.

- *Rousseau, Jean-Jacques.*

    - Emile, or About Education.

    - The Social Contract.

    - Letter to Christopher de Beaumont, Archbishop of Paris.

    - Letters Written from a Mountain.

    - Julia, or the New Heloïse.

- *Sabatier, Paul.*

    - Life of St. Francis of Assisi.

- *Saintyves, P.*

    - The Intellectual Reform of the Clergy and the Freedom of

      Education.

- The Saints as Successors of the Gods.

- Miracles and Historical Criticism.

- Miracles and Scientific Criticism.

- *Sand, George* (pseudonym).

  - All novels.

-

Schell, Hermann.

  - Catholic Dogma (Katholische Dogmatik).

  - Catholicism as a Principle of Progress.

  - The Divine Truth of Christianity.

  - The New Time and the Old Faith.

- *Seymour, Michael H.*

    - A Pilgrimage to Rome.

- *Soulié, Frédéric.*

    - All novels.

- *Stendhal, H.B. de.*

    - All novels.

- *Sterne, Laurence.*

    - A Sentimental Journey.

- *Strauss, David F.*

    - The Life of Christ.

- *Stroud, William.*

- Treatise on the Physical Cause of the Death of Christ.

- *Sue, Eugène.*

  - All novels.

- *Taine, H.-A.*

  - A History of English Literature.

- *Tolstoy, Dmitry.*

  - Roman Catholicism in Russia.

-

  Vericour, L.R. de.

  - Historical Analysis of Christian Civilization.

- *Viollet, Paul.*

- The Infallibility of the Pope and the Syllabus.

- *Vogrinec, Anton.*

  - Nostra maxima culpa (Our Greatest Fault).

- *Voltaire, F.-M. Arouet.*

  - Practically all his works.

- *Whateley, Richard.*

  - Elements of Logic.

- *White, Thomas.*

  - All works.

- *Wiese, Sigismund.*

  - Jesus (drama).

- *Zola, Emile.*

  - All works.